# EXPLORER TRAVEL GUIDES

# POLAR REGIONS

Charlotte Guillain

Raintree

Raintree is an imprint of Capstone Global Library Limited, a company incorporated in England and Wales having its registered office at 7 Pilgrim Street, London, EC4V 6LB – Registered company number: 6695582

www.raintreepublishers.co.uk
myorders@raintreepublishers.co.uk

Edited by Adam Miller, Laura Knowles, and Claire Throp
Designed by Steve Mead
Original illustrations © Capstone Global Library Ltd 2014
Illustrated by H L Studios
Picture research by Tracy Cummins
Production by Victoria Fitzgerald
Originated by Capstone Global Library Ltd
Printed in China by China Translation and Printing Services

ISBN 978 1 406 26013 7 (hardback)
17 16 15 14 13
10 9 8 7 6 5 4 3 2 1

ISBN 978 1 406 26020 5 (paperback)
18 17 16 15 14
10 9 8 7 6 5 4 3 2 1

**British Library Cataloguing in Publication Data**
Guillain, Charlotte
Polar regions. – (Explorer travel guides)
910.9'11-dc23
A full catalogue record for this book is available from the British Library.

**Acknowledgements**
We would like to thank the following for permission to reproduce photographs: Corbis p. 39 (© Ocean); Getty Images pp. 13 (Hulton Archive), 17 (Michael Sewell Visual Pursuit), 20 (Popperfoto), 22 (Rick Price), 26 (Darrell Gulin); Kate Bass p. 34 (© Kate Bass); Newscom p. 14 (Lieutenant Henry Bowers/AFP/Getty Images), 18 (Rick MacWilliam/Edmonton Journal/Canwest/MCT), 19 (ZUMA Press); Norwegian Polar Institute p. 28 (© Nick Cobbing); Photo Researchers, Inc. p. 30 (Lawrence Migdale); Shutterstock pp. 5 bottom, 24 (© Gentoo Multimedia Ltd), 5 middle, 9 (© Volodymyr Goinyk), 5 top, 6 (© Tyler Olson), 27 (© CampCrazy Photography); Superstock pp. 10, 25 (© Michael S. Nolan/age fotostock), 11, 37 (© Minden Pictures), 15 (© Image Asset Management Ltd), 23 (© Wolfgang Kaehler), 31 (© Kerstin Langenberger/ imagebroker.net), 33 (© Don Paulson Photography /Purestock).

Design elements: Shutterstock (© Khrushchev Georgy Ivanovich), (© Nik Merkulov), (© vovan), (© SmileStudio), (© Petrov Stanislav Eduardovich), (© Nataliia Natykach), (© Phecsone).

Cover photograph of a chinstrap penguin in Antarctica reproduced with permission of Getty Images (David W. Hamilton).

We would like to thank Daniel Block for his invaluable help in the preparation of this book.

Every effort has been made to contact copyright holders of material reproduced in this book. Any omissions will be rectified in subsequent printings if notice is given to the publisher.

# CONTENTS

Some words are shown in bold, **like this**. You can find out what they mean by looking in the glossary.

## Don't forget

These boxes will give you handy tips and remind you what to take on your polar adventures.

## Amazing facts

Check out these boxes for amazing polar region facts and figures.

## Who's who

Find out more about polar region experts and explorers of the past.

## Conservation

Learn about conservation issues relating to the polar regions.

# WELCOME TO THE POLAR REGIONS!

So, you're planning to visit the Arctic and Antarctic? Prepare yourself for the trip of a lifetime. This journey is only for the most daring explorers and the going will be tough. But you will experience stunning landscapes, unique wildlife, and some of the most extreme places on the planet!

## The Antarctic

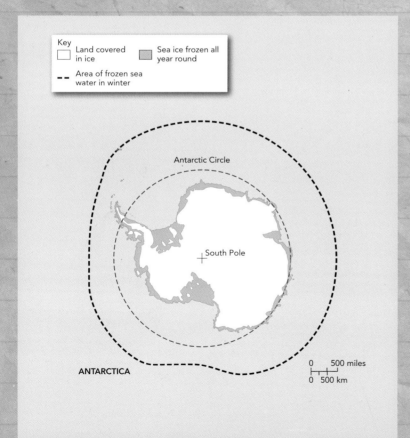

**Key**
☐ Land covered in ice
▨ Sea ice frozen all year round
- - Area of frozen sea water in winter

Antarctic Circle

+ South Pole

ANTARCTICA

0    500 miles
0    500 km

This map shows how the winter sea ice spreads out beyond the Antarctic Circle.

## From the top to the bottom

First stop is the Arctic, the region at the top of Earth's northern hemisphere. The North Pole is the point at the very top. Most of the Arctic is made up of the frozen Arctic Ocean and it's extremely cold all year round, especially in winter.

From there you'll travel to the opposite side of Earth, to Antarctica in the southern hemisphere. Antarctica is a huge landmass covered in a very thick ice sheet and it's the coldest place on the planet. The South Pole is as far south as you can go.

 ## Amazing facts

If you visit one of the polar regions during its winter, it will be completely dark, as the Sun's light cannot reach this part of Earth at this time. If you go during summer, the Sun will never set, so it will be light all the time.

## Turn the page...

See pages 6–7 to learn more about the Arctic.

Find out more about the ice in Antarctica on pages 8 and 9.

See page 24 to read about birds unique to Antarctica.

# BEFORE YOU GO

Before you set off on your trip, there are some important facts you need to know about the polar regions. With this information at your fingertips, you'll have a much safer and more exciting visit.

Spitzbergen Island, which is part of Norway, is in the Arctic.

## What is the Arctic?

The Arctic is made up of frozen ocean and frozen land. For hundreds of kilometres around the North Pole, there is nothing but the Arctic Ocean. This extremely cold ocean is covered with ice that can be up to 3 metres (10 feet) thick. In winter, the ice is twice as large as in summer, when the ice cracks and melts in the south of the Arctic. Part of the ice then breaks up into chunks of sea ice, called **floes**.

The southernmost part of the Arctic region is made up of land in North America, Europe, and Asia. The land closest to the Arctic Ocean is the polar desert, which is frozen rocky soil. South of this are dry plains called the **tundra**. In much of the tundra, the soil is frozen all year round. This frozen layer of soil is called **permafrost**. Trees cannot grow here, but some plants manage to survive. Also in the Arctic is the world's largest island, Greenland, which is mainly covered in a large ice sheet, called a **glacier**.

Forests lie south of the tundra, made up of **conifer** trees that can live in very cold temperatures. This large forested region is called the **taiga**.

## Amazing facts

The word *Arctic* comes from the ancient Greek word *arktos*. It means "bear", which is the name for a **constellation** of stars that can be seen in the northern sky.

# How did Antarctica form?

While the Arctic is a region made up of frozen ocean surrounded by frozen land, Antarctica is a huge frozen landmass called a **continent**. It is around 14 million square kilometres (5.4 million square miles), making it larger than the United States, Europe, or Australia. Scientists think this massive landmass was once part of a giant supercontinent called Gondwanaland, which broke apart hundreds of millions of years ago to form smaller continents. To begin with, Antarctica was not covered with ice and many living things survived there, but around 38 million years ago the continent began to freeze.

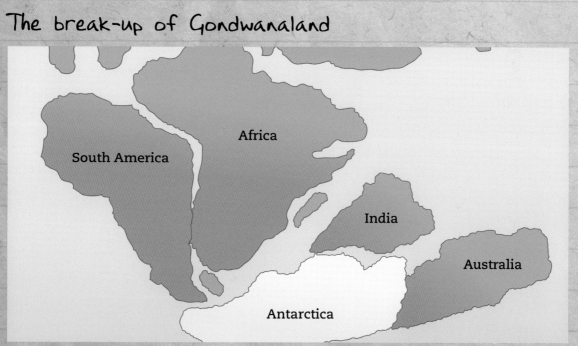

**The break-up of Gondwanaland**

This is how Gondwanaland broke up to make South America, Antarctica, Australia, Africa, and India.

# Frozen land and sea

Most of the dry, rocky land in Antarctica is covered in two sheets of ice. One sheet of ice covers the high **plateau** of East Antarctica and the other covers the mountains and islands of West Antarctica, with the Transantarctic Mountains in between. Other mountains and rocky peaks, called **nunataks**, stick up out of the ice in places, but many more mountains, lakes, and valleys are buried under the ice.

The Southern Ocean around Antarctica is also frozen for much of the year. The sea ice extends during the winter and cracks and melts in summer, creating ice floes.

These penguins survive on the rocky coast of Antarctica.

 # Conservation

The ice in Antarctica is the largest body of fresh water on Earth. The ice sheets contain 70 per cent of the world's fresh water. If the temperature in Antarctica becomes too warm, this ice could melt, causing oceans to rise and flood many coastal areas all over the world.

# On arrival

You won't have seen landscapes like these on your travels before!
On arrival in the Arctic you'll probably stay in a city, as humans have
settled across the south of the region. The largest city is Murmansk,
in Russia, which lies between the taiga and tundra. Moving further
north, settlements become smaller until only a few scientific research
stations are found. The only human settlements in Antarctica are
research bases for scientists. A few thousand people live there in
summer, with only a few hundred remaining in winter.

The Russian city of Murmansk is located close to the Barents Sea.

## Amazing facts

Glaciers are huge bodies of compressed ice and snow, formed
from fresh water. They are found in both polar regions.

## Stunning landscapes

The Arctic and Antarctica are made up of huge wilderness areas, covered in ice and snow. You'll find nunataks in both regions. In the Arctic, look out for Greenland's highest mountain, Gunnbjörns Fjeld, at 3,693 metres (12,116 feet). The tallest mountain in Antarctica is Mount Vinson at 4,892 metres (16,050 feet).

## Amazing facts

The Bentley Subglacial Trench in Antarctica is 2,555 metres (8,382 feet) below sea level and is the lowest place on Earth not covered by sea.

The first climbers reached the top of Mount Vinson in 1966.

## Icebergs

There are many icebergs in the Arctic, but the biggest are in Antarctica – some are as big as small countries! Icebergs form when layers of ice break off an ice sheet or glacier and float into the ocean. Only a fraction of an iceberg is visible above the water. These floating islands of ice offer a place to rest for many sea birds and mammals.

# THE FIRST EXPLORERS

Throughout history, the polar regions have captured the imaginations of explorers. You are following in some famous footsteps!

When Europeans discovered North America in the 1400s, a search began for the **Northwest Passage**, a way around the continent through which they could sail to Asia instead of travelling around Africa. They began to explore some of the Arctic in the process.

## Race to the North Pole

By the mid-1800s, explorers wanted to travel to the North Pole. No human had been there before. **Expeditions** from different countries began to race each other to reach the pole.

American explorer Robert Peary claimed to have reached the pole in 1909. He worked with Matthew Henson, an African-American engineer, who spent a lot of time with Inuit people, learning their skills and knowledge. Henson and four Inuit men were with Peary when he planted the US flag at the North Pole. But before Peary returned home, a fellow American explorer, Frederick Cook, said that he had reached the North Pole in 1908. To this day, nobody is sure who was first or if either team really reached the pole.

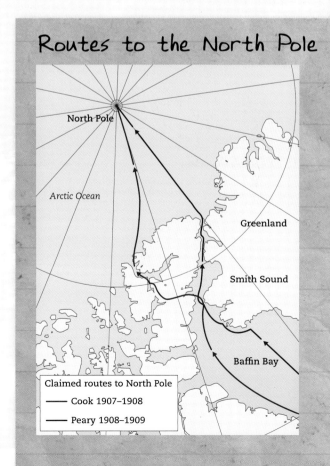

Routes to the North Pole

North Pole

Arctic Ocean

Greenland

Smith Sound

Baffin Bay

Claimed routes to North Pole
—— Cook 1907–1908
—— Peary 1908–1909

# Who's who

Robert Peary (1856–1920) was born in Pennsylvania, USA. He worked as an engineer in the US Navy and enjoyed exploring the Arctic during his holidays. He convinced people that his team had beaten Cook to the North Pole.

Frederick Cook (1865–1940) was a doctor from New York. He worked as a surgeon on an expedition to the Arctic with Peary in 1891. Cook couldn't prove he had reached the North Pole in 1908 but many historians think he was treated unfairly.

American explorer Robert Peary is seen here with his huskies.

British explorer Robert Falcon Scott (standing, centre) led an expedition to the South Pole in 1912.

## Exploring the Antarctic

Sailors first saw Antarctica in 1820. After this, explorers began to sail along the coast until expeditions landed at the beginning of the 1900s. British explorers Ernest Shackleton and Robert Scott visited Antarctica three times between 1901 and 1913. Expeditions faced great difficulties, especially when the sea froze and trapped their ships for months! By 1911, the race was on to reach the South Pole.

## Who's who

Robert Falcon Scott (1868–1912) was a naval officer who led an Antarctic expedition in 1899. The team had little experience but learned a lot, and discovered the Polar Plateau. Scott became a hero and his next challenge was the South Pole. Sadly, he was not as well prepared as Roald Amundsen (see next page) and lost the race to the Norwegian before losing his life.

# Triumph and tragedy

Robert Scott and his team set off for the South Pole in 1911. They took ponies and pulled sledges themselves but their route and the conditions proved to be too tough. When they reached the South Pole on 17 January 1912, they discovered that a Norwegian expedition, led by Roald Amundsen, had arrived on 14 December 1911. Sadly, Scott's team all died on the return journey.

## Who's who

In 1903, Norwegian doctor Roald Amundsen (1872–1928) led the first expedition to travel through the Northwest Passage in the Arctic. Amundsen (on the left in the photo below) learned useful survival skills, such as using dogs to pull sleds and wearing animal skins. After reaching the South Pole, Amundsen said "Victory awaits him who has everything in order."

# THE ARCTIC PEOPLE

Make sure you get to know some of the people who live in the Arctic when you visit. Different groups settled in the Arctic region about 1,000 years ago and about 4 million people live in the Arctic today.

## Where indigenous peoples live in the Arctic

USA
Canada
Arctic Circle
Russia
Greenland
Finland
Sweden
Norway

**Key**

| | |
|---|---|
| Indo-European family | Isolated languages |
| Uralic family | Eskimo-Aleut family |
| Altaic family | Na-Dene family |
| Chukotko-Kamchatkan family | |

## Arctic cultures

There are many different groups of people living in the Arctic, each with their own languages and **cultures**. Traditionally, most of these groups were herders or hunter-gatherers, who moved around and lived on the fish and animals they caught or herded, along with berries and plants they found in summer. They depended on animals such as seals and reindeer to provide **hides** for warm clothing.

Life has changed for many Arctic communities, although some still live in traditional ways. Many Inuit and Aleut people live in modern towns in Alaska, USA, and northern Canada. Some still have the skills to build igloos as shelter when they hunt far from home.

Several groups of people live in Siberia, including the Chukchi in the east, who hunt sea mammals. The Northern Samoyedic peoples include the Nenets, who depend on the herds of reindeer they keep for all their needs.

Saami people in the north of Norway, Sweden, and Finland also herd reindeer and fish along the coast. Saami people wear distinctive clothing called gákti, which uses colour and patterns to tell you about the person and their family.

These Inuit people are hunting whales.

# What's going on?

Visit the Arctic during March and you might catch the Arctic Winter Games. This event is held every two years to celebrate sporting and cultural achievements. The games include sports such as skiing, skating, and ice hockey, as well as special Arctic sports, such as sledge jump and Alaskan high kick. Arts, crafts, and music are also showcased.

These people are taking part in the Arctic Winter Games in Alberta, Canada.

# Who works here?

In both the Arctic and Antarctica, you might meet people who have moved there to work. **Conservationists** work to protect the environment and wildlife. Other scientists and **geologists** study Earth's **atmosphere** and **climate** change, among other things.

Some geologists are looking for oil and gas in the Arctic. Many local people support this because it could help their economies to grow. However, others worry about damage to the environment. Antarctica is protected by the Antarctic **Treaty**, which prevents companies from exploring for **minerals**. The treaty also ensures that scientists from around the world cooperate and share their research on Antarctica.

## Tourism

You'll soon notice you're not the only visitor to the polar regions! In Antarctica, the number of tourists grew from fewer than 9,000 in 1992 to over 46,000 in 2008. Because the environment in the polar regions is so fragile and unique, many tour companies make sure their visits work alongside conservation efforts, respect local cultures, and leave no waste or **pollution**.

Most people who live in Antarctica are doing scientific research at research stations like this one, but plumbers, electricians, and mechanics are also needed to make sure the research stations keep working.

# WHO'S GOING WITH YOU?

You won't be travelling to these extreme regions on your own. Here are some people who might be useful on your expedition.

## Expedition member: Ernest Shackleton (1874–1922)

Shackleton was an Irish explorer who visited Antarctica at the start of the 20th century. He worked with Robert Scott and travelled close to the South Pole. He's remembered as a hero for rescuing his crew when they were stuck in the winter ice.

**Why take him?** He'll always be there to save you if you get in trouble.

## Expedition member: Thomasie Sivuarapik

Thomasie Sivuarapik works at an Arctic survival training centre. He's an Inuit expert in polar survival. If you need to fish, hunt, or travel by dog sled to survive in the polar wilderness, Thomasie will help you out.

**Why take him?** He'll help you through some of the most extreme conditions on the planet.

## Expedition member: Kathryn Schaffer Miknaitis

Kathryn is an American scientist who helped to build the South Pole telescope during the summer of 2007 to 2008. Kathryn and her team had to work fast before winter arrived. By 2008, astronomers were able to use the telescope to study the universe.

**Why take her?** She can teach you about the Antarctic as well as the universe beyond our planet.

## Expedition member: Sir David Attenborough (born 1926)

Sir David has worked for the BBC since 1952, travelling around the world to make television programmes about nature. He visited the Arctic and Antarctica while making the series *Frozen Planet*, and has reached the North and South Poles.

**Why take him?** He will have lots to tell you about the wildlife you see on your trip.

# PLANTS AND WILDLIFE

You might not expect to see many plants growing in such cold, bleak places. However, you can spot plant life if you know when and where to look.

Purple saxifrage provides bright colour in the Arctic summer.

## Arctic blooms

During the brief Arctic summer, flowers suddenly appear on the tundra. These include the wild crocus, blue-spiked lupine, and saxifrage. They tend to grow on short stems to protect the flowers from the wind.

Other plant life can be seen in the Arctic, such as **lichens**, **mosses**, **algae**, grasses, and shrubs. These plants also grow close to the ground or shelter in rock crevices. They offer valuable food to many of the animals living in the Arctic, who **forage** for roots, shoots, and berries.

## Plants in Antarctica

The much colder conditions in Antarctica make it harder for any plants to survive. It is also very dry and the windiest place on the planet, so you won't be visiting any gardens! However, you might be surprised to learn that plant life does exist in this region.

Mosses are the most common type of plant here – look out for them on rocks, especially along the coast. You should also see algae in the snow and ice and lichens of many different colours growing on rocks. You might even spot Antarctica's only two flowering plants: Antarctic hair grass and Antarctic pearlwort.

Lichens cover many rocks in Antarctica.

# Unique birds

When you visit Antarctica you will definitely want to see penguins. The male emperor penguin keeps the egg laid by his female mate warm by tucking it close to his body, over his feet. The males huddle together through the freezing winter before the chicks hatch. Smaller Adélie penguins build nests out of rocks. The parents take turns to keep their egg warm. Penguins move slowly on land, but they can slide quickly on the ice and are amazing swimmers.

Pairs of emperor penguins take turns to look after their chick.

Flying birds in Antarctica include the snow petrel and South Polar skua. Snow petrels breed further south than any other flying bird and rely on the rocky nunataks for bare rock to build their nests. You might also spot the wandering albatross, with its huge wingspan, or Arctic terns that have flown down from the Arctic!

## Don't forget

You'll need a magnifying glass to spot some of the land animals that live in Antarctica. Mites, lice, fleas, and midges live on Antarctic birds and seals. Tiny insects called springtails also live under stones.

# Life in the Southern Ocean

The Southern Ocean around Antarctica is full of life. The sea here is full of krill, which is food to many ocean creatures, including the southern right whale, the blue whale, and the humpback whale. You might also see killer whales hunting seals, fish, and penguins. Keep a look out for Weddell, crabeater, leopard, and Ross seals peeping out of the water or lying on ice floes. Deep in the ocean, there are many **species** of fish that have adapted to live in cold water.

Many species of whale spend some of the year feeding in Antarctica.

# Arctic animals

The most famous Arctic animal is the polar bear. This huge, deadly **predator** is the largest carnivore on land and is perfectly equipped for life in the freezing north. The bear's heavy coat and thick layer of fat keep it warm, while its white fur provides camouflage as it hunts in the snow.

Other large Arctic animals include caribou, reindeer, and musk oxen. Their hooves are specially adapted to not slip on the ice. Wolves, Arctic foxes, wolverines, and hares can also be seen.

# Under the Arctic Ocean

For more incredible animals, just look in the water. See if you can spot a white beluga whale, killer whale, or a narwhal with its long spiralled tusk. If you're lucky, you might see a rare bowhead whale or blue whale.

Polar bears mainly hunt seals.

Look out for harp, bearded, or hooded seals as well as walruses that **haul out** of the sea onto the ice.

## Birds of the Arctic

Most of the birds in the Arctic **migrate** south during the winter and come back in summer. These include the redpoll, pipit, wheatear, Lapland longspur, and many ducks and geese. The snowy owl stays all year round. Its white feathers help it to hunt unseen by **prey**. Seabirds found in the Arctic include auks, Arctic terns, and herring gulls.

# Don't forget

You'll need sunglasses to look for wildlife on the ice. The white landscape can be blinding when the Sun shines. Remember your binoculars, too!

Beluga whales are also known as white whales because of their colour.

# INTERVIEW WITH A POLAR BEAR EXPERT

← Dr Jon Aars is a Research Scientist at the Norwegian Polar Institute. The Institute is concerned with researching and monitoring the Arctic and Antarctic environments.

**Q:** How did you become interested in polar bears?

**A:** I have always been interested in mammals. I started working with polar bears because that was the first job studying mammals that I applied for! My interest in polar bears has naturally grown as I have worked with them.

**Q: What does your work involve?**

**A**: I have been responsible for the polar bear research programme at the Norwegian Polar Institute since 2003. We collect samples and data in the field to use in a wide range of projects, for example studies of habitat use, disease, population size, and responses to human disturbance.

**Q: How much time do you spend in the Arctic and what do you do there?**

**A**: I spend one to two months in the Arctic every year, mostly in spring. We track polar bears and put them down using tranquilizer darts so we can mark them and take samples from them, such as blood and fat, to assess their health.

**Q: Why is the work you do so important?**

**A**: The work is very important because good knowledge about polar bears' biology may help save the bears in the future.

**Q: What advice would you give to someone who wants to study wildlife in the Arctic?**

**A**: To study wildlife in the Arctic, the main things you need are warm clothes and dedication.

# WEATHER AND CLIMATE

Make sure you think carefully about when you visit the polar regions. You can only travel to Antarctica during its summer (November to March) – if you stay later than April then you'll be stuck for the long, dark winter. It's also best to visit the Arctic during its summer (June to September), as during the darkness of winter many animals burrow into holes or dens under the snow or migrate to warmer places.

## Sightseeing tip

One reason to visit the Arctic in winter is to see the Aurora Borealis, or northern lights. Electrically-charged particles from the Sun enter Earth's atmosphere and produce colourful, swirling lights in the sky.

These Inupiat people live in Alaska.

The long Arctic winter can be bleak.

## Arctic climate

Arctic winters are long and very cold, while the summer is short and cool. In the far north, the Arctic stays frozen all year round, while further south the ice melts during summer. Temperatures vary, but during summer the average temperature is 10 degrees Celsius (50 degrees Fahrenheit), while in winter this plummets to -40 degrees Celsius (-40 degrees Fahrenheit). Snow falls all year round, although it can rain in some areas during the summer.

## Antarctic climate

The lowest ever recorded temperature in nature of -89.2 degrees Celsius (-129 degrees Fahrenheit) was measured in Antarctica. At the South Pole, the average summer temperature is -30 degrees Celsius (-22 degrees Fahrenheit), while in winter temperatures average around -60 degrees Celsius (-76 degrees Fahrenheit). It is extremely dry, with very little snowfall. Scientists have recorded wind speeds in Antarctica of 327 kilometres (203 miles) per hour.

# Climate change

For many years, scientists have been measuring temperatures across the world. The climate is changing all over the planet and in the polar regions temperatures are rising. This means that sea ice is melting and during the polar summers less and less ice is remaining. In the Arctic, the amount of sea ice has decreased by 2.9 per cent every ten years since 1979. In Antarctica, the change is less dramatic but the amount of overall sea ice is decreasing.

## Conservation

The penguins of Antarctica are being affected by climate change. Over the last 50 years, the number of emperor penguins in Antarctica has halved. As the sea ice shrinks, the penguins' habitat gets smaller, making it harder for them to raise their chicks.

Scientists expect that temperatures in the Arctic will rise two or three times more than in the rest of the world. Even a small rise in temperature could make the ice in the Arctic melt. Polar bears would no longer be able to hunt on the ice for seals and the oceans would rise around the world. If the ice sheet in Antarctica melted, sea levels around the world could rise as much as 60 metres (197 feet).

## Don't forget

It's very important to stay warm in the polar regions:
- Always cover your head and wrap up your face.
- Wear layers to stay warm but remove some layers if you start to sweat, or the moisture will get into your clothes and freeze later.
- Make sure your outer layer is windproof and waterproof.
- Wear thin gloves under thick mittens.

Large chunks of ice fall off icebergs as they melt.
This is called calving.

# INTERVIEW WITH A CLIMATE SCIENTIST

← Dr John King is the Science Leader in the Climate Programme at the British Antarctic Survey.

**Q:** How did you become a climate scientist?

**A**: I've always had an interest in the natural world, and particularly in the weather. When I was nine years old, I set up my own **weather station** at home. I studied physics at university and went on to do a PhD in **meteorology**. I had always been a keen mountaineer and loved wild, remote places, so when I got a chance to do field work in Antarctica with the British Antarctic Survey I jumped at the opportunity! I've been working on the weather and climate of the polar regions ever since.

**Q:** How much time do you spend in Antarctica and what do you do there?

**A**: When I first went to Antarctica, I would spend two to three months away from home, making measurements at one of our Antarctic stations. Nowadays, most of my time is spent at BAS headquarters in Cambridge, making use of measurements that other people have made.

We have people who spend the whole year at our Antarctic stations, making regular **observations** of the weather from instruments at the stations and using instruments carried by balloons launched from the stations. During the Antarctic summer, we also make measurements of the atmosphere from a special aircraft.

## Q: Why is the work you do so important?

**A**: We know that the polar regions are a very important part of the natural environment. They are home to many much-loved creatures, such as penguins in Antarctica and polar bears in the Arctic. Climate change in the polar regions can pose a threat to these species. Polar climate change also has consequences for all of us. For example, warming in Antarctica and Greenland could cause parts of the polar ice sheets to melt, raising sea levels and making flooding more likely in low-lying coastal areas. If we want to understand these risks, we need to know how polar climate may change into the future.

## Q: What do you love most about your job?

**A**: I love trying to puzzle out how weather and climate work and why we are seeing the changes that we see in the polar regions. It's a bit like being a detective, trying to solve a crime mystery with just a handful of clues.

## Q: What advice would you give to someone who wants to be a climate scientist?

**A**: Spend lots of time outside. Look around and ask yourself questions – why is it pouring with rain today when yesterday was hot and dry? Find out about climate in other parts of the world – why is it different from the climate where you live? A good scientist needs to be curious.

# BE A GOOD TOURIST!

Now you have researched the polar regions, you will understand how special the Arctic and Antarctic are. While many people are keen to visit these unique places, it is important for visitors to remember that any tourism could damage these beautiful and important environments.

## The Antarctic Treaty

The Antarctic Treaty has been signed by 46 countries and is designed to protect Antarctica. Part of this involves ensuring tourism does not damage the region. All travel companies taking tourists to Antarctica have to make sure their trip is safe and does not harm the environment. Tourists are encouraged to learn about the research that is done in Antarctica and many take part in conservation work while they are there. No waste or pollution is left behind.

 **Conservation**

In many ways, the best thing you can do to help the polar regions is not to visit them! Exploring the Arctic and Antarctic by reading books and websites won't damage these special places at all. If you do decide to visit, find out about a research or conservation project you can help with during your visit and tell your family and friends all about it on your return.

# Don't forget

## Tourism in the Arctic

Visitors to the Arctic are also encouraged to take care of the environment and its inhabitants. Make sure you:

- find out as much information about the Arctic as you can before you go

- try to stay in places where your visit will bring **income** to local people

- learn a little of the local language

- don't disturb wild animals or plants and never leave litter.

These tourists are exploring Antarctica by ship.

# Trip of a lifetime

So now you're ready to explore the polar regions and discover more about these wonderful places. What are you looking forward to seeing or experiencing the most?

## Don't forget

Make sure you take a camera to take photos of your trip. If you want to keep a diary as you explore you'd better take a pencil, as most normal pens will freeze in the cold temperatures. And you can forget about using a mobile phone because there will be no signal! If you want to call home while you're away then you will need to pack a satellite phone.

# Protect the polar regions

The Arctic and Antarctica are under threat. Not only is climate change causing the sea ice and glaciers to melt, but human activity could also disrupt these regions. Some countries want to mine for **natural resources** and minerals, such as coal, **iron ore**, copper, and oil in Antarctica. Mining is already taking place in the Arctic. These industries bring pollution, waste materials, and oil and chemical spills, all of which can harm wildlife and damage the environment. Tourism in the polar regions can also interfere with the delicate natural balance.

Make sure you use your trip to the polar regions to learn as much as you can about these incredible places. Remember to share what you discover with as many other people as possible.

Many people are worried about the damage oil companies could cause in the Arctic.

 # Conservation

When you've seen polar bears and penguins in the wild you will want to protect them more than ever. You can help to do this by supporting organizations such as the World Wildlife Fund, which **campaign** to save these animals' habitats and raise awareness about climate change.

# WORLD MAP

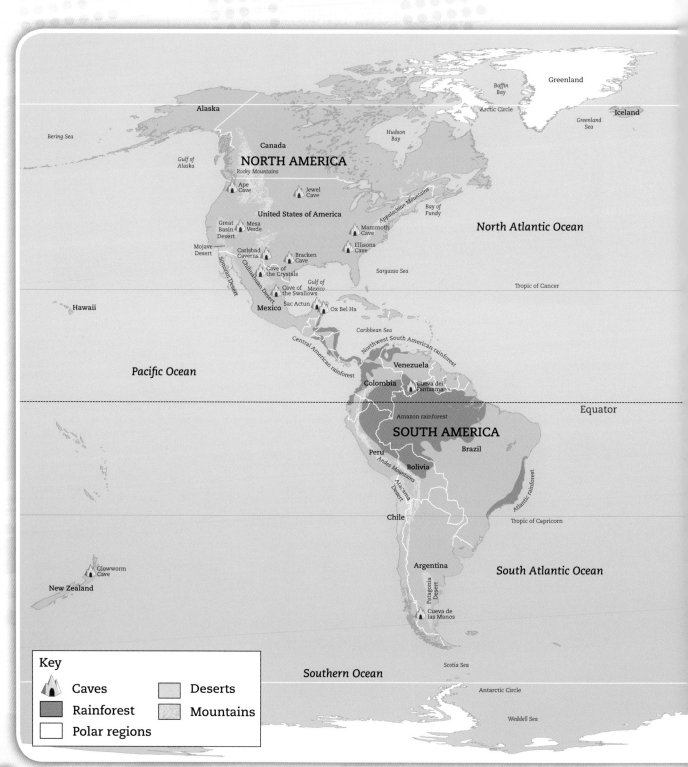

Greenland

Baffin
Bay

Arctic Circle

Iceland

Greenland
Sea

Alaska

Bering Sea

Hudson
Bay

Gulf of
Alaska

Canada

**NORTH AMERICA**

Rocky Mountains

Ape
Cave

Jewel
Cave

Bay of
Fundy

North Atlantic Ocean

**United States of America**

Great
Basin
Desert

Mesa
Verde

Mammoth
Cave

Appalachian Mountains

Mojave
Desert

Carlsbad
Caverns

Bracken
Cave

Ellisons
Cave

Cave of
the Crystals

Sargasso Sea

Tropic of Cancer

Cave of
the Swallows

Gulf of
Mexico

Hawaii

Mexico

Sac Actun

Ox Bel Ha

Caribbean Sea

Central American rainforest

Northwest South American rainforest

Venezuela

Pacific Ocean

Colombia

Cueva del
Fantasma

Amazon rainforest

Equator

**SOUTH AMERICA**

Peru

Brazil

Andes Mountains

Bolivia

Atacama
Desert

Atlantic rainforest

Chile

Tropic of Capricorn

Argentina

South Atlantic Ocean

Patagonia
Desert

Glowworm
Cave

New Zealand

Cueva de
las Manos

Scotia Sea

Southern Ocean

Antarctic Circle

Weddell Sea

## Key

Caves

Deserts

Rainforest

Mountains

Polar regions

This map shows where the polar regions are. Why not explore the oceans, caves, mountains, deserts, and rainforests also shown on the map?

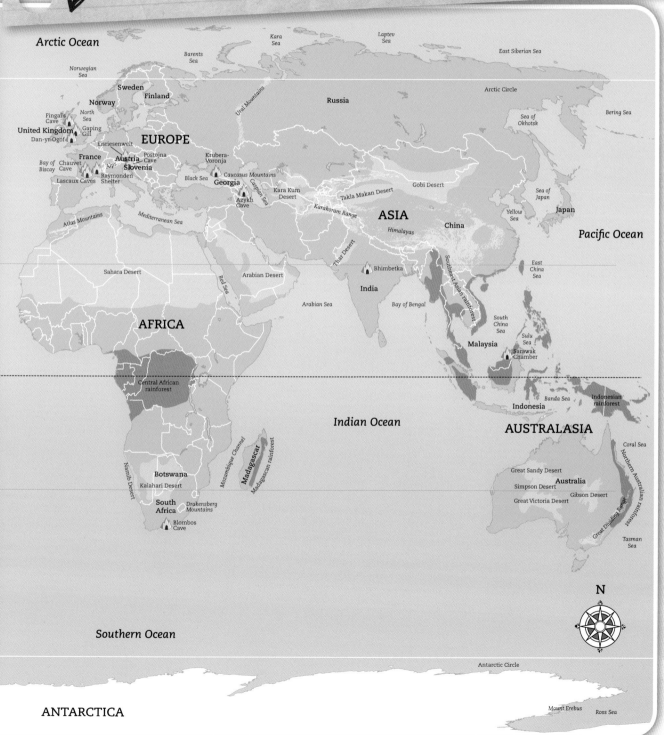

Arctic Ocean

Kara Sea
Barents Sea
Laptev Sea
East Siberian Sea
Norwegian Sea
Arctic Circle
Sweden
Finland
Norway
North Sea
Russia
Sea of Okhotsk
Bering Sea
Fingal's Cave
United Kingdom
Gaping Gill
Dan-yr-Ogof
EUROPE
Eisriesenwelt
Postojna Cave
Krubera-Voronja
Ural Mountains
France
Austria
Slovenia
Chauvet Cave
Bay of Biscay
Alps
Raymonden Shelter
Black Sea
Caucasus Mountains
Georgia
Lascaux Caves
Azykh Cave
Caspian Sea
Kara Kum Desert
Takla Makan Desert
Gobi Desert
Sea of Japan
Japan
Atlas Mountains
Mediterranean Sea
ASIA
Himalayas
China
Yellow Sea
Pacific Ocean
East China Sea
Sahara Desert
Red Sea
Arabian Desert
Thar Desert
Bhimbetka
India
Arabian Sea
Bay of Bengal
Southeast Asian rainforest
South China Sea
AFRICA
Malaysia
Sulu Sea
Sarawak Chamber
Central African rainforest
Banda Sea
Indonesia
Indonesian rainforest
AUSTRALASIA
Indian Ocean
Coral Sea
Mozambique Channel
Madagascar
Madagascan rainforest
Northern Australian rainforest
Namib Desert
Botswana
Kalahari Desert
Great Sandy Desert
Australia
Simpson Desert
Gibson Desert
South Africa
Drakensberg Mountains
Great Victoria Desert
Great Dividing Range
Blombos Cave
Tasman Sea

N

Southern Ocean

Antarctic Circle

ANTARCTICA

Mount Erebus
Ross Sea

# TIMELINE

| | |
|---|---|
| 1400s | European sailors start to search for the Northwest Passage and begin to explore the Arctic |
| 1773 | James Cook crosses the Antarctic Circle |
| 1820 | Sailors first see Antarctica |
| 1840s | Separate British, US, and French expeditions confirm that Antarctica is a continent |
| 1878 | Baron Nordenskiöld from Finland completes the first successful journey through the Northwest Passage |
| 1901 | A team of British explorers, including Ernest Shackleton and Robert Scott, visit Antarctica |
| 1906 | Roald Amundsen successfully travels through the Northwest Passage in the Arctic |
| 1908 | Frederick Cook claims to reach the North Pole |
| 1909 | Robert Peary claims to reach the North Pole |
| 1911 | Roald Amundsen reaches the South Pole |
| 1959 | The Antarctic Treaty is signed |
| 1969 | The Arctic Winter Games are founded |
| 2008 | Astronomers start using the South Pole telescope |
| 2008 | Polar bears are listed as a threatened species |
| 2012 | Oil companies start drilling in the Arctic |
| 2012 | British explorer Sir Ranulph Fiennes announces plans to travel across the Antarctic on foot during the Antarctic winter of 2013 |

# FACT FILE

## ARCTIC

| Size: | 30 million square kilometres (11.5 million square miles) |
|---|---|
| Population: | around 4 million people |
| Largest settlement: | Murmansk |
| Average summer temperature: | 10°C (50°F) |
| Average winter temperature: | -40°C (-40°F) |
| Lowest ever recorded temperature: | -67.8°C (-94°F) |
| Highest point: | Gunnbjörns Fjeld at 3,693 metres (12,116 feet) |

## ANTARCTICA

| Size: | 14 million square kilometres (5.4 million square miles) |
|---|---|
| Population: | a few thousand in summer reducing to a few hundred in winter |
| Largest settlement: | US Antarctic Program's McMurdo Station |
| Average summer temperature: | -30°C (-22°F) |
| Average winter temperature: | -60°C (-76°F) |
| Lowest ever recorded temperature: | -89.2°C (-129°F) |
| Highest point: | Mount Vinson at 4,892 metres (16,050 feet) |

# GLOSSARY

**algae** simple plant-like living things, for example seaweed

**atmosphere** layer of gases surrounding Earth, made of a mixture of gases that humans and living things need to breathe

**campaign** take part in activities to spread a message or ask for change

**climate** general weather conditions in a region over time

**conifer** tree with leaves like needles that do not fall off in autumn, and that grows cones

**conservationist** person who works to protect natural environments

**constellation** group of stars

**continent** large land mass

**culture** practices, beliefs, and traditions of a society

**expedition** trip made to explore or discover a place or thing

**floe** small chunk of floating ice

**forage** search for food

**geologist** person who studies the rocks and minerals in the ground

**glacier** large mass of slow-moving ice

**Global Positioning System (GPS)** device that uses satellite signals to pinpoint the user's exact position

**haul out** when sea mammals, such as seals and walruses, leave the water to rest on land or ice

**hide** skin of an animal

**income** money coming into a household or community

**indigenous** people who originated in the place they now live

**iron ore** rock in the ground containing iron

**lichen** simple plant that grows on rocks and tree trunks

**meteorology** study of the weather

**migrate** move from one place to another at certain times of year

**mineral** naturally occurring substance that is found under ground

**moss** small green plants that grow in damp places

**natural resources** materials found in nature that people can use

**Northwest Passage** journey by sea along the northern coast of North America from the Atlantic Ocean to the Pacific Ocean

**nunatak** peak of rock surrounded by snow and ice

**observation** watching carefully to get information

**permafrost** ground that is permanently frozen

**plateau** large, flat area of highland

**pollution** damage in the environment caused by human-made waste

**predator** animal that hunts and kills other animals for food

**prey** animal that is killed by another animal for food

**scurvy** disease caused by a lack of vitamin C

**species** type of animal

**supplement** tablet containing the vitamins and minerals that might be missing in someone's diet

**taiga** swampy forest to the south of the Arctic

**treaty** agreement between two or more countries

**tundra** large, flat area in the Arctic with permanently frozen soil

**weather station** place with instruments to study the weather

# FIND OUT MORE

## Books

*Arctic*, Lorrie Mack (Dorling Kindersley, 2007)

*Arctic and Antarctic* (DK Eye Wonder), Lorrie Mack (Dorling Kindersley, 2006)

*Polar Regions*, Steve Parker (QED, 2008)

*Polar Survival*, Jen Green (Miles Kelly Publishing, 2012)

## Websites

**www.bbc.co.uk/nature/places/Antarctica**

Visit the BBC Nature website to find out more about animals in the polar regions. Scroll down the page to find the link to information about the Arctic.

**gowild.wwf.org.uk/polar**

The World Wildlife Fund (WWF) website has information about the conservation of polar animals.

**kids.nationalgeographic.com/kids/animals/creaturefeature**

Find out about the animals living in Arctic and Antarctic habitats.

**www.nhm.ac.uk/nature-online/earth/antarctica**

The Natural History Museum's website has a section about Antarctica.

# Places to visit

### The Polar Museum

Scott Polar Research Institute

University of Cambridge

www.spri.cam.ac.uk/museum

Visit the museum to see artefacts from polar expeditions of the past and learn what scientists are doing in the polar regions today.

### Discovery Point

Discovery Quay

Dundee

www.rrsdiscovery.com

Visit Captain Scott's ship *Discovery* to find out about his explorations.

### The Oates Museum

Selborne Hill

Selborne

Hampshire GU34 3BN

www.gilbertwhiteshouse.org.uk

Visit the Oates Museum to find out about Captain Lawrence Oates, who died on the South Pole expedition led by Captain Scott in 1912.

# Organizations

### British Antarctic Survey

www.antarctica.ac.uk

The BAS is a leading scientific research centre, studying the environment in Antarctica.

### World Wildlife Fund

www.wwf.org.uk

The WWF campaigns to protect wildlife in the polar regions and the natural environments there.

EXPLORER **TRAVEL** GUIDES

# INDEX